Revised

Exploring English 2

Workbook

Dr Usha Ram

Collins

Revised

Exploring English 2

Workbook

r Usha Ram

Acknowledgements

The authors and publishers wish to acknowledge the authors listed below, and thank the following for permission to use copyright material.

I'm Seven from *Collins Big Cat: Mind the Gap* © Roger McGough 2012, is printed by permission of United Agents (www.unitedagents.co.uk) on behalf of Roger McGough; *Collins Big Cat: Chewy Hughie* reprinted by permission of HarperCollins Publishers © 2006 Jane Clarke; *Collins Big Cat: Brown Bear and Wilbur Wolf* reprinted by permission of HarperCollins Publishers © 2012 Sarah Parry; *Collins Big Cat: The Singing Beetle* reprinted by permission of HarperCollins Publishers © 2011 Linda Strachan.

Every effort has been made to trace copyright holders and to obtain their permission for the use of copyright material. The authors and publishers will gladly receive any information enabling them to rectify any error or omission in subsequent editions.

Illustrations

Unit 1: *I'm Seven*, Natalie Kilany; Test 1: *Chewy Hughie*, Sarah McConnell; Unit 4: *Brown Bear and Wilbur Wolf*, Judy Musselle; Test 2: *The Singing Beetle*, Oliver Hurst. All other illustrations Richa Kinra, Priyankar Gupta, Ajit Narayan, Q2A Media Services Private Limited and Danish Zaidi.

Cover: Olga_Bonitas, Evgeniya_m, Askold Romanov

Title Page: Olga_Bonitas, Evgeniya_m, Askold Romanov

Photographs

p20: &#169 Joachim Angeltun, Askold Romanov; p27: Bubert; p41: colematt; p47: JFLangton; p48: Lyllyflow; p53: joaquin croxatto; p55: memoangeles; p58: Tigatelu, yayayoyo, kbeis; p66: yelet

Published by Collins India
A division of HarperCollins*Publishers* India Private Limited

HarperCollins *Publishers*
A-75, Sector 57, Noida, Uttar Pradesh 201301, India
1 London Bridge Street, London SE1 9GF, United Kingdom
2 Bloor Street East, Toronto, Ontario M4W 1A8, Canada
Lvl 13, 201 Elizabeth Street (PO Box A565, NSW, 1235),
Sydney NSW 2000, Australia
195 Broadway, New York, NY 10007, USA

Browse the complete Collins catalogue at
www.collins.in

First edition 2015
Latest revised edition 2018

Reprint: 10 9 8 7 6 5 4 3 2 1

ISBN: 978-93-5277-143-1

Typesetting and page layout by Q2A Media Services Private Limited,
Recto Graphics

Cover layout by Rahul Dhiman

Printed and bound in India by MicroPrints (India), New Delhi

PREFACE

Revised Exploring English is a multi-skill course in English, designed for children and young people growing up in a world of global communication. It aims to develop their cognitive abilities, train them to think critically and communicate effectively in a wide variety of contexts. It adheres to the latest National Curriculum Framework. The series has been revised and updated based on detailed user feedback.

Built around salient themes, the units in the book comprise carefully selected reading texts authored by Indian and global writers. They cater to a variety of student interests and needs, motivate engagement and promote critical thinking. Through the reading of the texts, learners are expected to develop as thinking individuals who are keenly aware of the world around them – linguistically competent, cognitively able and morally responsible.

The eight-level series includes coursebooks, workbooks and literature readers for levels 3 to 8. Each level is also accompanied by a comprehensive Teacher's Resource Book and digital resources for the teacher in the form of an interactive DVD.

Workbooks 1 – 5

The workbooks are mapped to the coursebooks and are designed to complement them by providing additional material for skills practice, review and assessment. The grammar sections give a short reminder of the main grammar point covered in the corresponding unit in the coursebook, and are followed by practice exercises to reinforce the language. There are also plentiful practice exercises to practice key vocabulary, language skills, reading and writing. The workbooks also contain Activity sections and Test sections, which can be implemented in the school year.

Coursebooks

Each Coursebook comprises ten units, each of which is based around a main reading passage. Each unit includes a *Warm-up* to stimulate the learners' interest. A carefully selected reading passage acts as a starting point for all language work and discussion throughout the unit. This is followed by *Comprehension*, *Vocabulary* and *Grammar* exercises, as well as *Listening*, *Speaking*, *Writing* and *Language skills* activities. There are also five poetry sections in each book, followed by *Poetry appreciation* and an *Activity* which allows learners to explore the topic further. In addition, two *Projects* and two *Life Skills* are provided at each level.

Literature Readers

The Literature Readers teach critical appreciation of literature through short stories, folktales and fairytales, extracts from quality literature and classic novels, and poems from various eras and regions. A range of text-types is covered, with learners' attention being drawn to the genre of each piece. Literary devices are also highlighted, with a glossary of literary terms at the end of each book.

Teacher's Resource Books

The Teacher's Resource Books contain model lesson plans, photocopiable worksheets covering all the pedagogical aspects included in the Coursebooks, answer keys to all exercises, along with extra analytical activity sheets.

Digital resources

The Collins DigiSuite DVD comprises:

1. **Enhanced e-book:** includes the coursebook in digital format with additional features like audio, animated poems, pronunciation help and interactive exercises.
2. **Test generator:** an easy-to-use tool to help teachers create tests with a few clicks.
3. **Teacher resources:** includes lesson plans, answer keys, listening texts, additional worksheets, further project ideas, and extra support with assessment.

We hope that the course will foster a love for reading in young learners and provide teachers with language acquisition tools that can be used to effectively impart communication skills and equip young minds with an awareness about the world.

CONTENTS

Unit 1 Worm Looks for Lunch **7**
Reading comprehension 7
Vocabulary 8
Grammar 9
Language skills 10
Writing 11

Unit 2 Annual Haircut Day **13**
Vocabulary 13
Grammar 14
Listening 15
Speaking 15
Writing 16

Unit 3 Little Mouse Bakes a Cake **17**
Vocabulary 17
Grammar 18
Writing 19

Unit 4 The Stone Cutter **21**
Reading comprehension 21
Vocabulary 22
Grammar 24
Writing 27

Unit 5 The Brave Baby **28**
Vocabulary 28
Grammar 29
Language skills 31
Writing 31

Activity 1 .... **33**
Listening 33
Speaking 34

Test 1 .... **35**

Unit 6 The Boy and the Drum **39**
Vocabulary 39
Grammar 40
Language skills 41
Listening 41
Speaking 42
Writing 42
Unit 7 The Shepherd Boy: Part 1 .... **43**
Vocabulary 43
Grammar 44
Listening 45
Speaking 46
Writing 46
Unit 8 The Shepherd Boy: Part 2 .... **47**
Vocabulary 47
Grammar 48
Language skills 49
Writing 50
Unit 9 A Busy Morning 52
Vocabulary 52
Grammar 53
Listening 55
Speaking 55
Writing 56
Unit 10 Here We Come **57**
Vocabulary 57
Grammar 58
Language skills 59
Writing 59
Activity 2 .... **60**
Listening 60
Speaking 61
Test 2 .... **62**

Unit 1

Worm Looks for Lunch

Reading comprehension

A **Read this poem about a child who is seven years old today.**

I'm Seven

I'm seven, I'm seven
I'll never be six again

I used to be five
And I used to be four

I'll never be three
Or two any more

I used to be one
But those days are long gone[1]

Next year I'll be eight
Then I'll be nine

And the year after that
I'll be ten

I'm seven, I'm seven
I'm in seventh heaven[2]
And I'll never be six again.

Roger McGough

Wordfile

1. **Long gone** means a long time ago in the past.
2. If you are in **seventh heaven**, you are very happy.

B Fill in the blanks with the correct words from the poem.

again   heaven   never   Next   to   used

1. The child ________ to be one.
2. The child will ________ be six again.
3. ________ year, the child will be eight.
4. The child used ________ be four.
5. The child will never be five ________.
6. The child is in seventh ________ (= is very happy).

Vocabulary

A Where do the animals live? Fill in the blanks with the correct words.

1. The dog sleeps in its k________.
2. The fish lives in the P________.
3. The bird is sitting in its n________.
4. The rabbit is in its b________.
5. The horse sleeps in its s________.
6. The deer walks across the g________.

B Circle the correct word to complete the sentences.

1. Lemons are very *sour/sweet*.
2. Yoghurt is very *hard/soft*.
3. This pizza is very *chewy/sweet*!
4. The bread is very *dry/sour*.
5. Sugar is *salty/sweet*.
6. Biscuits are *hard/sour*.

Grammar

Remember!

I like/I do not like/Do you like?

- When we think a thing or a person enjoyable or interesting, we like it.

  I like *football.* ***I like*** *my grandmother.*

- When we don't think a thing or a person enjoyable or interesting, we do not like it.

  I do not like *cheese.* ***I do not like*** *injections.*

- When we ask someone what he or she finds interesting, we begin the question with 'Do you like ...'

  Do you like *swimming?* ***Do you like*** *chocolates?*

A Fill in the blanks with the correct words.

carrots Do eating like not playing shopping you

1. __________ you like cheese?
2. We __________ chocolate.
3. I like __________ kulfi.
4. I do __________ like fish.
5. Do __________ like rice and dal?
6. I like __________, but I do not like peas.
7. Do you like __________ cricket?
8. They like to go __________.

Remember!

- When we talk about the things another person does, we add **s** or **es** to the doing word.

*I **read** the newspaper.*	*She **reads** the newspaper.*
*I **sing** a song.*	*He **sings** a song.*

B **Choose the correct words to fill in the blanks.**

1. The shop ______________ (*open/opens*) at ten in the morning.
2. My sister ______________ (*play/plays*) guitar.
3. My father ______________ (*go/goes*) for jogging in the morning.
4. He always ______________ (*say/says*) the truth.
5. Ana ______________ (*sing/sings*) very well.

Language skills

Write the words for these things in the correct column.

1. 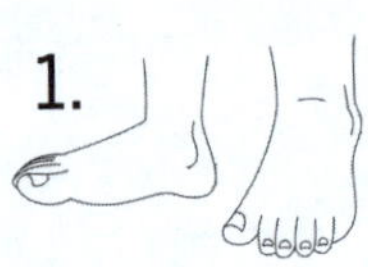

3. 

5. 

2. 

4. 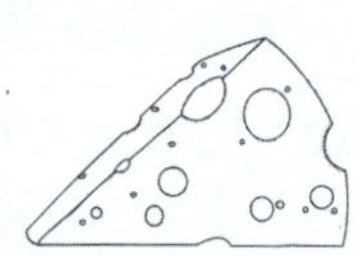

6. 

ea	ee

Writing

A Complete the sentences using the pictures to help you.

1.  I ____________________ carrots.

2.  Do you ____________________ apples?

3. 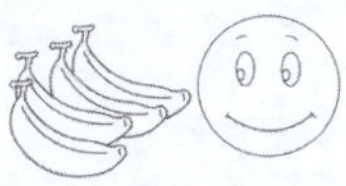 I ____________________ bananas.

4. 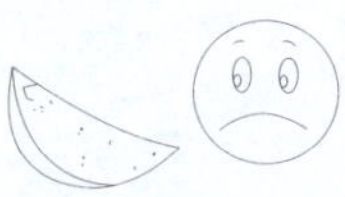 I ____________________ melon.

5. 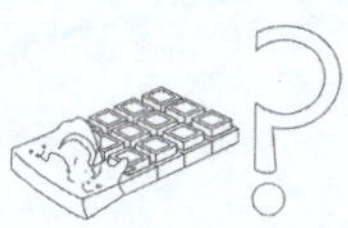 ____________________ you ____________________ chocolate?

6.  I ____________________ rice.

B Draw your favourite food and drink. Write five sentences about the food and drink.

____

____

____

____

____

____

____

C **Write a conversation about food or drink. Use the pictures below or use your own ideas.**

1.

2.

Unit 2 Annual Haircut Day

Vocabulary

A Match the beginning of each sentence with its ending.

1. My mum is angry
2. My sister is worried
3. I am scared
4. When I am with my friends,
5. It is very late and I
6. I am sad because it is the end

a. about her exams.
b. of the holiday.
c. I feel happy.
d. feel sleepy.
e. with me.
f. of spiders.

B Rearrange the capital letters and fill in the blanks.

1. Raj is very __________ (LTAL). He has __________ (HOSTR), black hair. He likes wearing a T-shirt and a pair of __________ (EJASN).

2. Mira has long, __________ (RULCY) hair. She often has a __________ (ILNYTAPO). She ties it up with a __________ (BBNORI).

Grammar

Remember!

Naming words: countable and uncountable

- Words for people, places, animals and things are **naming words**.
- Some naming words can be counted. They are **countable**.

  chair → chairs *dot → dots* *table → tables*
- Some naming words cannot be counted. They are **uncountable**.

  milk *oil* *rice* *sugar*
- Uncountable words cannot be plural. So, we cannot say ~~waters~~ or ~~sugars~~. We always use them in their singular form.

  Do you like milk? *Yes, and I also like orange juice.*

A **Circle the five naming words.**

air angry book Bhutan buy children clay

Charlie dal eat hair house Priti see

shop sleepy Taj Mahal truck wood

B **Are these countable or uncountable? Circle C for countable and U for uncountable.**

1. apple juice C/U
2. anger C/U
3. ball C/U
4. bread C/U
5. box C/U
6. dog C/U
7. hairbrush C/U
8. rain C/U
9. rice C/U
10. sugar C/U

Listening

Listen to Shilpa talking about her sister. Are the sentences true or false? Circle T or F.

1. Neha is very tall. T/F
2. She has big eyes. T/F
3. She has wavy hair. T/F
4. She never brushes her hair. T/F
5. She is usually happy. T/F
6. She is scared of all animals. T/F

Speaking

Work with a partner. Take turns to read a sentence from the left. Your partner must give the correct answer from the right.

1. I need to wash my hair.
2. I need to dry my hair.
3. I need to comb my hair.

a. OK, here is the towel.

b. OK, here is the comb.

c. OK, here is the shampoo.

Writing

A **Think of three people in your family. Describe their hair.**

My grandmother has short, grey hair.

1. ______________________________

2. ______________________________

3. ______________________________

B **Imagine you have a new haircut. Draw a picture of your new hairstyle. Write a sentence about it.**

____

Unit 3 Little Mouse Bakes a Cake

Vocabulary

A Match the cooking words with the pictures.

1. 
2. 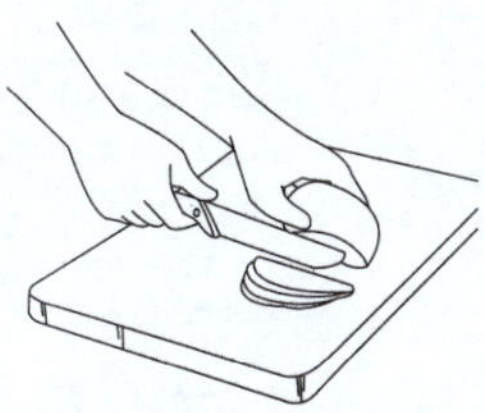
3. 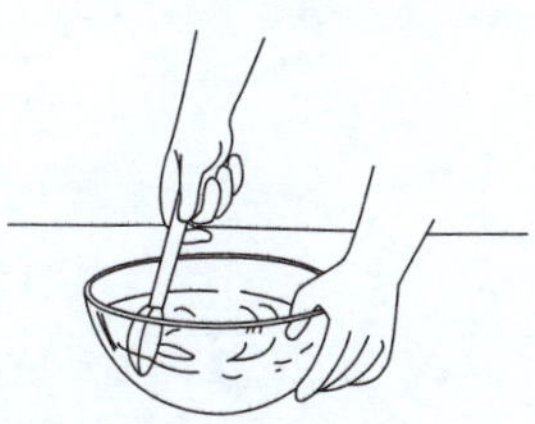
4. 
5. 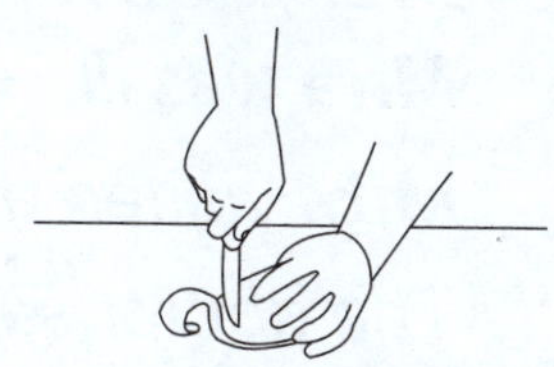
6. 

a. to add
b. to boil
c. to chop
d. to fry
e. to mix together
f. to peel

B Fill in the blanks with the correct words.

bake	bowl	cut	mixture	Pour	stir

1. Put the butter and the sugar into a big ________.
2. Put the bread in the oven and ________ it for thirty minutes.
3. Put the ________ into a bowl.
4. Take two apples and ________ them into small pieces.
5. Put the mixture into a big bowl and ________ it until it is smooth.
6. ________ the cream into a pan.

Grammar

Remember!

Subject and object pronouns

- A **pronoun** is a word that takes the place of a noun.
- We use **I**, **she**, **he**, **we**, **they** and **it** for replacing a noun that does the action.
- We use **me**, **you**, **her**, **him**, **us**, **them** and **it** for replacing a noun that receives the action.

__Mita__ was ill. → __She__ was ill.

__Mita__ visited a doctor. → __She__ visited a doctor.

The doctor saved __Mita__. → The doctor saved __her__.

A Tick (✓) the correct sentence from each pair.

1. a. I love baking.
   b. Me like baking.
2. a. Swati baked a cake for I on my birthday.
   b. Swati baked a cake for me on my birthday.
3. a. The shopkeeper gave she a pen.
   b. The shopkeeper gave her a pen.
4. a. The teacher punished them.
   b. The teacher punished they.
5. a. The boy is absent because he is sick.
   b. The boy is absent because him is sick.

B **Circle the correct word to complete each sentence.**

1. Wash the cherries and then put *it/them* in a bowl.
2. Put the sauce in a bowl and then stir *it/them*.
3. Could you give *I/me* that spoon, please?
4. Can *I/me* help you with the cooking?
5. Aslam and Feroze would like a sandwich. *Them/They* are hungry.
6. Will you let *us/we* have pizza tonight?
7. *Us/We* bought fresh fruits for our salad.
8. What lovely cakes! Did you make *them/they*?
9. Sameera made pasta for *I/me*.
10. *Us/We* prepared the dinner together.

Writing

A **Write suitable words to complete the sentences from recipes.**

banana butter cake cream flour fruit ice cream mixture

1. Pour cream on top of the fruit.
2. Bake the ________ in a hot oven for an hour.
3. Put the ________ and the ________ in a bowl and mix them together.
4. Chop the ________ into small pieces and put on top of the ________.
5. Take the ________ out of the oven and cut it into pieces.
6. Stir the ________ until it is smooth.

B **Here are some pictures of the things we need to make a sandwich. Look at the ingredients and write the recipe for a sandwich.**

Reading comprehension

A **Read this story about a bear and a wolf.**

Brown Bear and Wilbur Wolf

Brown Bear was hungry after sleeping all winter. He came out of his den to find food. But he could not smell anything.

He went into the forest to look for berries[1]. But he could not smell anything.

He went to the river to look for fish. But he could not smell anything.

Brown Bear was sad. 'I have lost my smell[2],' he cried. 'How will I find food?'

The birds saw Brown Bear and they flew down to play with him. Brown Bear was happy and he jumped.

But the birds got a fright[3] and flew away.

A rabbit saw Brown Bear in the field and he went to play with him. Brown Bear was happy. He ran towards the rabbit.

But the rabbit got a fright and ran into a hole.

Brown Bear lay down in the grass. He was lonely and he was still hungry.

Wilbur Wolf came out of the forest. He was hungry too.

He saw Brown Bear. 'Hello, Bear! I am old and weak. Will you help me find food?'

'I am sorry,' said Brown Bear. 'I have lost my smell. I cannot help you find food.' They were both sad.

Then Brown Bear had an idea. 'Let us find food together. I am strong and you have your smell. So you can find food and I will catch it!' he said.

So Brown Bear and Wilbur Wolf became friends. They found berries and caught fish together. They were never hungry again.

Sarah Parry

Wordfile

1. **Berries** are small, round fruits that grow on plants and trees.
2. Here, **my smell** refers to the sense of smell.
3. If you **get a fright** (at something) you are afraid of it.

B Number the sentences in the correct order.

☐ Brown Bear lay down in the grass and was hungry.

☐ Brown Bear and Wilbur Wolf went to look for food together.

☐ Brown Bear went to the forest and the river, but he did not find food.

☐ The birds and a rabbit joined Brown Bear, but they were afraid of him.

☐ Brown Bear came out of his den.

☐ Wilbur Wolf came to speak to Brown Bear.

Vocabulary

A Circle the correct describing word to complete each sentence.

1. A child who has no friends may feel *hungry/lonely*.
2. People often smile when they are *happy/sad*.
3. I sometimes cry when I am *sad/strong*.
4. We need to eat food when we are *hungry/lonely*.
5. When you are ill, you often feel *strong/weak*.
6. A person who can pick up heavy things is *happy/strong*.

B **Rearrange the capital letters to write the names of jobs. Match the words to the pictures.**

1. LEECARN cleaner
2. TCODRO ________
3. MERFRA ________
4. SREIHRDARES ________
5. HERTACE ________
6. TONES ERTUCT ________

a. 

b. 

c. 

d. 

e. 

f. 

C **Fill in the blanks with the correct words.**

1. A teacher writes on a b________ with a chalk.
2. A hairdresser cuts your hair with a pair of s________.
3. A cleaner cleans the room with a b________.
4. A doctor checks your temperature with a t________.
5. A farmer digs his farms with a s________.
6. A stone cutter uses a h________ and c________ to cut the rock.

Grammar

Remember!

a, an and the

- The first time something is mentioned, we use **a** or **an**.

  I bought ***a*** *book on dinosaurs from the book fair.*
- After that, we use **the**.

  I liked ***the*** *book. It has many pictures.*
- If there is only one of something, we always use **the**.

  Look at ***the*** *moon.*

  The *sun is very hot today.*

  I visited ***the*** *Mughal Gardens in New Delhi.*

  The *capital city of China is Beijing.*

A Are the underlined words in these sentences correct or wrong? Circle C (correct) or W (wrong).

1. Look at the moon tonight – it's beautiful! C/W
2. New Delhi is a capital city of India. C/W
3. There is a beautiful bird in that tree over there. C/W
4. We went to see a Taj Mahal. C/W
5. Aslam gave me an apple. C/W
6. This is the centre of the town. C/W
7. He lives in a new house. C/W
8. Who is the President of India? C/W

B Circle the correct word to complete each sentence.

1. Would you like *a/an* ice-cream, Ameena?
2. A potato is *a/the* vegetable.
3. My father works in a bank and my mother is *a/the* teacher.
4. Never look at *a/the* sun.
5. We saw *a/an* horse.
6. They wanted to buy *an/the* car, but it was too costly.
7. We stayed in *a/an* friendly hotel in Ooti.
8. I liked *a/the* book you gave me.

Remember!

-*ing* words for talking about the weather

- We can use words with ***-ing*** to talk about the weather.
  *It is rain**ing** in France.*
- We take away the 'e' when we add ***-ing***.
  move → *mov**ing***

C Fill in the blanks with the correct words from the box.

falling	is	It	moving	shining	wind

1. ________ is raining.
2. The ________ is blowing.
3. The clouds are ________.
4. It ________ snowing.
5. The sun is ________.
6. The leaves are ________.

D **Write a sentence from Exercise C next to each picture.**

1.  ____________ ____________ ____________

2.  ____________ ____________ ____________

3.  ____________ ____________ ____________

4.  ____________ ____________ ____________

E **What is Swati doing? Write sentences using *-ing* words and the words in the box. Remember to take away the 'e'.**

call her mother	choose a cake	dance	drive	have breakfast	write a letter

1. She is writing a letter.
2. She is ____________.
3. She is ____________.
4. She ____________.
5. She ____________.
6. She ____________.

1. 

2. 

3. 

4. 

5. 

6. 

Writing

A **Colour the picture.**

B **Now write five sentences to describe the picture.**

1. ______________________________

2. ______________________________

3. ______________________________

4. ______________________________

5. ______________________________

• Unit 5

The Brave Baby

Vocabulary

A Match the words with their descriptions.

1. cottage
2. tent
3. palace
4. apartment
5. caravan
6. bungalow

a. a large house that is joined to another house on either side

b. a very large house where a king or a queen lives

c. a set of rooms for living in, usually on one floor and part of a larger building

d. a large vehicle that is pulled by a car and is used for living in

e. a small house, usually in the country

f. a shelter made of cloth that is held up by poles and ropes, usually used for camping

B Circle the correct words to complete the sentences.

1. We go to the library to *play/read/shout*.
2. When I am very happy, I *grin/hurry/like*.
3. I go to the baker when I *enjoy/like/want* to buy bread.
4. When something is funny, I *cry/giggle/step*.
5. I often *call/hurry/shout* my friends at the weekend.
6. When people are pleased, they *cry/like/smile*.

Grammar

Remember!

Yesterday words

- We know that **yesterday words** are used to talk about things that happened in the past, and are finished now.

  *The chief was **surprised**.* *Wasso **smiled** at him.*

- We add ***-ed*** to the end of most doing words to make yesterday words.

  *She **looked** up at the chief.* *The chief **danced** and **danced**.*

A Make yesterday words from the today words in the box. Use them to fill in the blanks.

bore	call	climb	cook	enjoy	like	open	play	walk	watch

1. Anil and Rakesh __________ football yesterday.
2. I __________ my friend to tell her about my new doll.
3. We __________ all the way to the beach.
4. My mother __________ fish for dinner.
5. I __________ the film very much.
6. Nazia __________ the window.
7. They __________ the mountain successfully.
8. Shonali and Risha __________ their picnic near the lake.
9. We __________ *The Jungle Book* together.
10. He felt __________ and decided to read a book.

B Where is the star? Write the correct position words.

behind between in front of next to on top of under

1. ______________

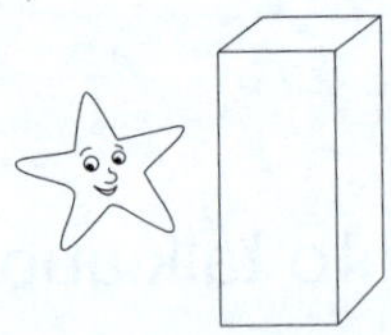

2. ______________

3. ______________

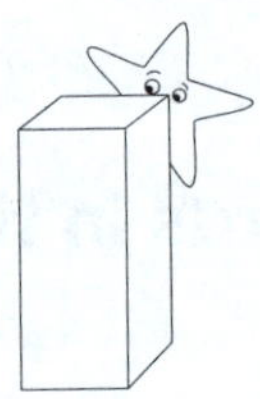

4. ______________

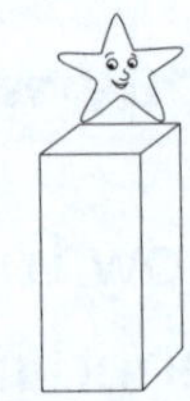

5. ______________

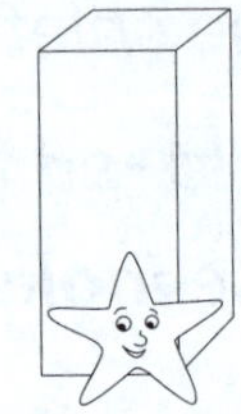

6. ______________

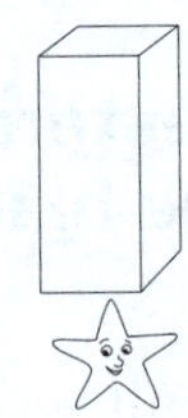

C Follow the instructions.

1. Draw a teddy on a chair.
2. Draw a vase of flowers on top of the bookcase.
3. Draw some DVDs on the floor in front of the TV.
4. Draw slippers under the sofa.
5. Draw a picture hanging on the wall.

Language skills

Remember!

Spelling: *-ied* words

- Doing words that end in a consonant followed by **y** (for example, ***cry***) end in ***-ied*** when they are in the past tense.

  cry → *The baby* ***cried****.*

  carry → *Mahesh* ***carried*** *the books for the teacher.*

Write the past tense of the doing words in brackets to complete the story about Nishi's day.

Yesterday morning I [1] __________ (hurry) to school because I was late.

At school, we [2] __________ (study) English and I learned some new words.

Then we had a maths lesson. I [3] __________ (try) to understand, but it was very difficult!

After school, I played tennis with my friend Kokila. In the evening, I [4] __________ (tidy) my bedroom.

Writing

A Write sentences about four things you did yesterday.

1. Yesterday I ______________________________.
2. Yesterday I ______________________________.
3. Yesterday I ______________________________.
4. Yesterday I ______________________________.

B **Imagine a conversation with a friend about what he or she did yesterday. Write the conversation. Use the pictures to help you or use your own ideas.**

You: ____

____

Your friend: ____

____

You: ____

____

Your friend: ____

____

You: ____

____

Activity 1

Listening

A Listen and match the sentence halves.

1. This coat is
2. That building is
3. Those biscuits are
4. This bread is
5. These pets are

a. too big for us.
b. all for me.
c. very strange.
d. too costly for me.
e. very hard.

B Listen and write the correct information in the box.

My best friend

Name: 1 ______________________

Age: 2 ______________________

Hair: long/short and 3 ______________________

Favourite things: cats, 4 ______________________

Favourite food: 5 ______________________

Favourite drink: 6 ______________________

Speaking

A Look at the words. Say words that rhyme with them.

1. hand
2. hat
3. hot
4. key
5. make
6. nest
7. rice
8. sad

B Look at the rows of pictures. Which picture doesn't fit in each row? Why?

1.

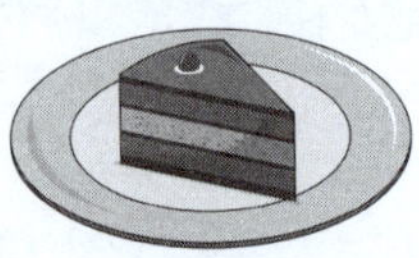
cake

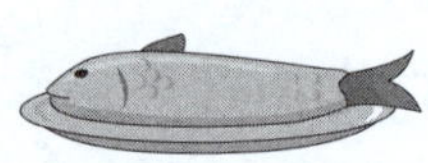
fish

milk

rice

2.

chair

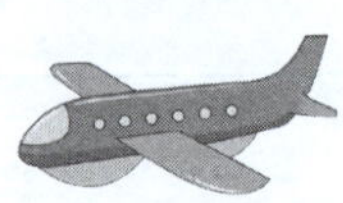
plane

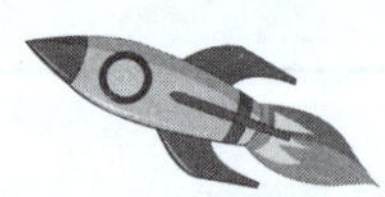
rocket

ship

3.

biscuits

cake

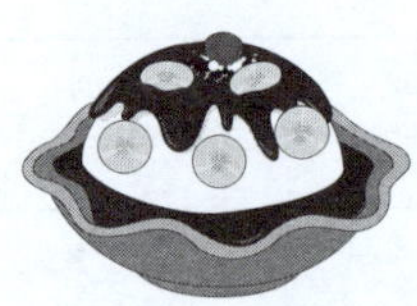
ice cream sundae

rice and dal

4.

cat

giraffe

monkey

tiger

Test 1

Reading comprehension

A **Read this poem about a pet dog called Hughie.**

Chewy Hughie

All Hughie does is chew, chew, chew.
Whatever are we going to do?
He chews up toys, he chews up bones.
He chews up shoes and mobile phones.

He chews the paper and the mail.
When Mum says, 'NO!', he wags his tail.
He chews the carpets and the doors.
Nothing is safe from Hughie's jaws.

He chews up Grandpa's stick and hat.
He tries to chew up Granny's cat.
Oh! Hughie's found some bubble gum
And now he's chewing it for fun.

All Hughie does is chew, chew, chew
And now his jaws are stuck like glue.
Chewy Hughie's in big trouble.
He's inside a huge, pink bubble.

Hughie! Hughie! You have to stop.
Don't chew, Hughie, or you'll go...
POP!

Jane Clarke

B **Choose the best answers.**

1. Hughie likes to chew
   a. things that taste good.   b. almost anything.
2. When Mum tells Hughie to stop chewing, he
   a. stops chewing things.   b. looks happy, then chews more things.
3. The poet would like Hughie
   a. to chew other things.   b. to stop chewing everything.
4. Grandpa and Granny are not pleased with Hughie because
   a. he chews their things.   b. he chews bubble gum.
5. At the end of the poem, Hughie is inside a huge, pink bubble made of
   a. bubble gum.   b. soap.

Coursebook comprehension

Answer the questions.

1. In 'Worm Looks for Lunch', what food does the worm like best?

   ____

   ____

2. In 'Annual Haircut Day', what happens when Sringeri Srinivas sees the tiger?

   ____

   ____

3. In the poem 'Boo!', what is the word that makes the girl brave?

____

____

4. In 'Little Mouse Bakes a Cake', why doesn't Mouse give any cake to Raven or Crane?

____

____

5. How many grasshoppers are there in the poem 'High June'?

____

____

6. In 'The Stone Cutter', why does the man choose to become a poor stone cutter again?

____

____

7. What time of the day is mentioned in the poem 'Listen'?

____

____

8. In 'The Brave Baby', what does the chief do to stop Wasso from crying?

____

____

Grammar

Circle the correct words to complete the sentences.

1. I *do not like/like* maths.
2. For my lunch, I only have *a apple/an apple*.
3. 'Can I have this apple?' – 'No, *he/it* is for Ravi.'
4. 'Do you like lassi?' – 'Yes, I love *it/them*.'
5. My cake is in *an oven/the oven*.
6. Would you like *a cup of tea/the cup of tea*?

Writing

Choose the best words to complete the conversation.

a glass | Do you like | I don't like | loves it | that banana | this soup

Mira: Mmm, 1______________ is very nice!

Mrs Shah: I often make it. Everyone 2______________.

Mira: May I have 3______________ of water, please?

Mrs Shah: Of course. And what shall we have for dessert? 4______________ fruit?

Mira: I like bananas, but 5______________ mangoes.

Mrs Shah: That's good. You can have 6______________ in the bowl.

Unit 6 The Boy and the Drum

Vocabulary

A Match the describing words with their opposite meanings.

1. small	a. quiet
2. loud	b. dry
3. tall	c. normal
4. wet	d. dirty
5. strange	e. big
6. clean	f. short

B Match the describing words to their meanings. Write P for positive words and N for negative words.

1. crazy	______	a. not ill
2. healthy	______	b. with too many people
3. attractive	______	c. may hurt you
4. crowded	______	d. at ease or relaxed
5. dangerous	______	e. very silly
6. popular	______	f. has lots of friends
7. comfortable	______	g. safe to eat
8. edible	______	h. nice to look at

Grammar

Remember!

Question words

- In the story, the boy asks questions such as:

  What *is the matter?* ***Why*** *are you sad?*

The words **what** and **why** are question words.

- Question words are used to ask questions. Some common question words are – **who**, **where**, **when**, **what** and **why**.

Put the words in the correct order to make questions. Remember to use question marks.

1. is that/over there/tall man/who

   ____

2. are you/quarrelling/with/why/your friend

   ____

3. cartoon/favourite /is your/ what

   ____

4. get over/will/when/your exams

   ____

5. are we/for/going/our holidays/where

   ____

6. is your/new/ teacher/Who

   ____

Language skills

Here are some sentences. Add the missing commas.

1. He needs cucumber tomato salt bread and cheese to make sandwiches.

   ____

2. There are three chairs one table one bed and a sofa in the room.

   ____

3. Aman invited Kavita Ali Mayan and Toni to his birthday party.

   ____

4. There were cakes biscuits candies and gifts lying on the table.

   ____

5. He can speak English Chinese Spanish and French fluently.

   ____

6. Nisha's dog likes to run swim and play.

   ____

Listening

Listen to the conversations and fill in the blanks with *lend* or *borrow*.

1. Can I ________ your pencil?
2. Can you ________ me your cycle for a day?
3. You haven't returned my book that you ________ last week.
4. Can you ________ me your dress?
5. Can I ________ your ball?

Speaking

Work with a partner. Put the words in the correct order to make questions. Take turns to ask and answer the questions.

1. breakfast/do/eat/for/What/you
2. and/brothers/do/have/How many/sisters/you
3. do/How/often/TV/watch/you
4. a hobby/Do/have/you
5. animal/favourite/is/What/your

Writing

Write a short letter to your friend, Brad, in America. Tell him about your life. Use the words in the box to help you.

always	my best friend is	often
at the weekend	my hobby is	sometimes

Dear Brad

Unit 7 The Shepherd Boy: Part 1

Vocabulary

A Complete the words to make sentences.

1. We use a s__________ to eat soup.
2. I use a k__________ to cut fruits and vegetable.
3. I cut a piece of paper with a pair of s__________.
4. We cook vegetables in a p__________.

B Where do you use these things? Write the words in the correct place.

hoe knife lawnmower oven pan shampoo soap spade spoon toothbrush towel watering can

kitchen	bathroom	garden

C Match the words to make compound words.

1. bath	a. cake
2. pan	b. bow
3. rain	c. tub

Grammar

Remember!

Joining words: and, but, so

- We use **and** to join two sentences together to make one sentence.

  The wolf stood on the rock. *It stared at the sheep.*

  → *The wolf stood on the rock **and** stared at the sheep.*

- We use **but** to join two sentences when we are surprised or annoyed.

  The sheep did nothing. *They ate grass all day long.*

  → *The sheep did nothing **but** ate grass all day long.*

- We use **so** to join two sentences where the second sentence shows a result.

  Lakhya had gone to town. *Nandu took the sheep out to graze.*

  → *Lakhya had gone to town **so** Nandu took the sheep out to graze.*

A Circle the correct word to complete the sentences.

1. It is raining *and/but/so* you need an umbrella.
2. I called Saba *and/but/so* asked her to help me.
3. I want to buy a book *and/but/so* I do not have any money.
4. You can walk to the village *and/but/so* it is a long way.
5. Feroze tidied his room *and/but/so* washed his clothes.
6. We do not have a ball *and/but/so* we cannot play football.
7. I am hungry *and/but/so* there is no food in the kitchen.
8. You have an exam tomorrow *and/but/so* you must study tonight.

B **Match the beginning of each sentence with its ending.**

1. Ashok was ill
2. I went to Toshili's house
3. I have two sisters
4. I don't have a pen
5. Fishes can swim
6. Farhan plays cricket
7. Seema was cold
8. We have a test on Monday
9. I need butter, milk
10. The dog saw him

a. and a brother.
b. and he also likes football.
c. but they can't fly.
d. so he went to the doctor.
e. and bread.
f. so we have to study together.
g. so she put on her jacket.
h. but I have lots of pencils.
i. and wagged its tail.
j. but she was not there.

Listening

Listen to what Raj says. Are the sentences true or false?

Circle T or F for each sentence.

1. T/F
2. T/F
3. T/F
4. T/F
5. T/F
6. T/F

Speaking

Work with a partner. One of you says what you want to do. The other says what you need. Use the words below.

I want to cook some soup.

You need a pan.

1. cut/paper/pair of scissors
2. clean/teeth/toothbrush
3. bag/carry/shopping
4. dig/garden/spade
5. eat/spoon/yoghurt
6. broom/floor/sweep

Writing

Write your own sentences about the objects you use to do things. Here are two examples:

I use a towel to dry my hair.

I use a pair of scissors to cut paper.

1. ____
2. ____
3. ____
4. ____
5. ____

Unit 8 The Shepherd Boy: Part 2

Vocabulary

A Fill in the blanks with the correct noise words.

1. The duck started to q__________.
2. The dog started to b__________.
3. The cow started to m__________.
4. The wolf started to h__________.
5. The bee started to b__________.
6. The lion started to r__________.
7. The sheep started to b__________.
8. The chicken started to c__________.
9. The mouse started to s__________.
10. The owl started to h__________.

B Fill in the blanks with the correct words.

comfortable easy greedy funny loud obedient safe straight

1. My brother likes __________ music.
2. Is it __________ to swim here?
3. This armchair is very __________.
4. My homework was __________.
5. The film was very __________.
6. Can you draw a __________ line?
7. Henry is an __________ student.
8. The children stared at the laddus with __________ eyes.

Grammar

Remember!

Describing words

- We use describing words to describe people, things and animals.

  *The day was **dark** and **gloomy**.*

  *The sun was **hot**.*

  *The wolf stared with **greedy** eyes.*

A Match the describing words with the naming words.

1. cold	a. friend
2. fierce	b. sky
3. comfortable	c. drink
4. blue	d. question
5. good	e. edge
6. difficult	f. sofa
7. tall	g. picture
8. fast	h. car
9. sharp	i. wolf
10. colourful	j. tree

B **Put the describing word in brackets into the correct place in each sentence.**

1. I have a very suitcase. (heavy)

 ____

2. My brother is very. (tall)

 ____

3. Her hair is and wavy. (long)

 ____

4. Raj is wearing a T-shirt. (red)

 ____

5. It is very this morning. (cold)

 ____

6. I eat lots of fruit. (fresh)

 ____

Language skills

Are the full stops and question marks in these sentences correct? Change them if they are not.

1. Do you like swimming. ______________
2. I have three sisters. ______________
3. I get up at six o'clock? ______________
4. What is your friend's name? ______________
5. Where is the station. ______________
6. The dog is very fierce. ______________
7. I have wavy hair? ______________
8. Why are you smiling. ______________

Writing

A Complete the sentences with a suitable describing word.

1. Delhi is a ____________ city.
2. My best friend has ____________ eyes.
3. English is ____________ to learn.
4. My bedroom has ____________ walls.
5. The soup is too ____________.
6. Elephants are ____________.

B Write two lists of describing words: one for you and one for someone else.

words that describe you	**words that describe ____________**
1. ____________	1. ____________
2. ____________	2. ____________
3. ____________	3. ____________
4. ____________	4. ____________
5. ____________	5. ____________
6. ____________	6. ____________

C **Draw a picture and write some sentences about yourself (how you look, what your character is like).**

D **Now draw a picture of the person from Exercise B. Write some sentences about him or her.**

Unit 9 A Busy Morning

Vocabulary

A Find the measure words in the box and fill in the blanks.

1. A ______________ of rice.
2. A ______________ of soup.
3. A ______________ of tea.
4. A ______________ of chocolate.
5. A ______________ of honey.
6. A ______________ of flour.
7. A ______________ of water.
8. A ______________ of bread.

B	A	Z	E	V	B	L	B	K	J
O	Q	A	B	N	Y	M	A	H	B
W	S	R	A	X	P	D	G	O	A
L	Q	N	R	Z	R	G	R	L	X
N	U	T	P	S	E	L	W	L	Z
T	A	B	L	O	A	F	O	O	N
J	T	D	E	G	L	A	S	S	M
A	G	R	A	I	N	U	Z	P	W
R	P	O	D	F	A	X	X	O	D
V	X	P	E	A	C	U	P	S	E

B Choose the correct option.

1. A ______________ of musicians.
   a. team b. band
2. A ______________ of keys.
   a. bunch b. pair
3. An ______________ of ants.
   a. army b. group
4. A ______________ of thieves.
   a. gang b. series
5. A ______________ of players.
   a. board b. team
6. A ______________ of grapes.
   a. bunch b. crew

Grammar

Remember!

my, your, his, her, its our and **their**

- Describing words such as **my**, **your**, **his**, **her**, **its**, **our** and **their** show that something belongs to someone.

__My__ bed is clean. *__Your__ bed is untidy.*

__His__ house is big. *__Her__ dress is new.*

__Our__ class is quiet. *__Their__ class is noisy.*

A Fill in the blanks with the correct form of words given in the brackets.

1. ____________ (they) mother is a teacher.
2. The door to ____________ (you) room is locked.
3. This is Sheila's dog. ____________ (it) name is Bob.
4. He loves reading. These are ____________ (he) books.
5. When will you return ____________ (me) playstation?
6. We are cleaning ____________ (we) shoes.

Remember!

always, never, often, sometimes

- We use **sometimes**, **often**, **always** and **never** to describe how many times we do something.

I __sometimes__ go to the zoo. *I __often__ go to the playground.*

I __always__ brush my teeth. *I __never__ eat meat.*

B **Put the words in the correct order to make sentences. Remember to use full stops and capital letters.**

1. Bela/eats/fish/never

____

2. play/often/Sara and Zoya/tennis together

____

3. Anil/father after/helps his/school/sometimes

____

4. chicken/for lunch/have/I/often

____

5. goes/never/Revathi/swimming

____

C **Answer this question about you. Tick (✓) your answers.**

1. How often do you exercise?

a. I exercise every day.	☐	c. I exercise sometimes.	☐
b. I exercise often.	☐	d. I never exercise.	☐

D **Tick (✓) the correct sentence from each pair.**

1. a. Fardeen never visits his uncle. ☐
   b. Fardeen visits his uncle never. ☐
2. a. Saif and Yusuf often meet after school. ☐
   b. Saif and Yusuf meet after school often. ☐
3. a. Jolly goes every Friday to his guitar lesson. ☐
   b. Jolly goes to his guitar lesson every Friday. ☐
4. a. Nishi helps often her brother with his homework. ☐
   b. Nishi often helps her brother with his homework. ☐
5. a. Pooja has sometimes lunch at the café. ☐
   b. Pooja sometimes has lunch at the café. ☐

Listening

Mona and her brother are going shopping. They want to buy something for their grandmother's birthday. Listen to them talking and fill in the blanks with the correct words.

1. Mona is going shopping with her brother, ____________.
2. It is their grandmother's ____________ birthday.
3. They order a big ____________ ____________ for her.
4. They also plan to buy a bouquet of ____________, which is grandmother's favourite flower.
5. Mohit decides to draw a ____________ for grandmother.

Speaking

Mona is at the bakery. She wants to order a birthday cake for their grandmother. Work with a partner and role-play the situation. Take turns to ask and answer questions.

Baker: Ask what kind of cake you want.

Mona: Order a birthday cake. Use the words below.

Use the words given below.

1. flavor of cake/size of cake
2. chocolate cake/1 kg
3. decoration/ message
4. Happy Birthday Granny
5. special candle/75 years

Writing

A Complete the word-web with the things Billy-Bob buys from the market.

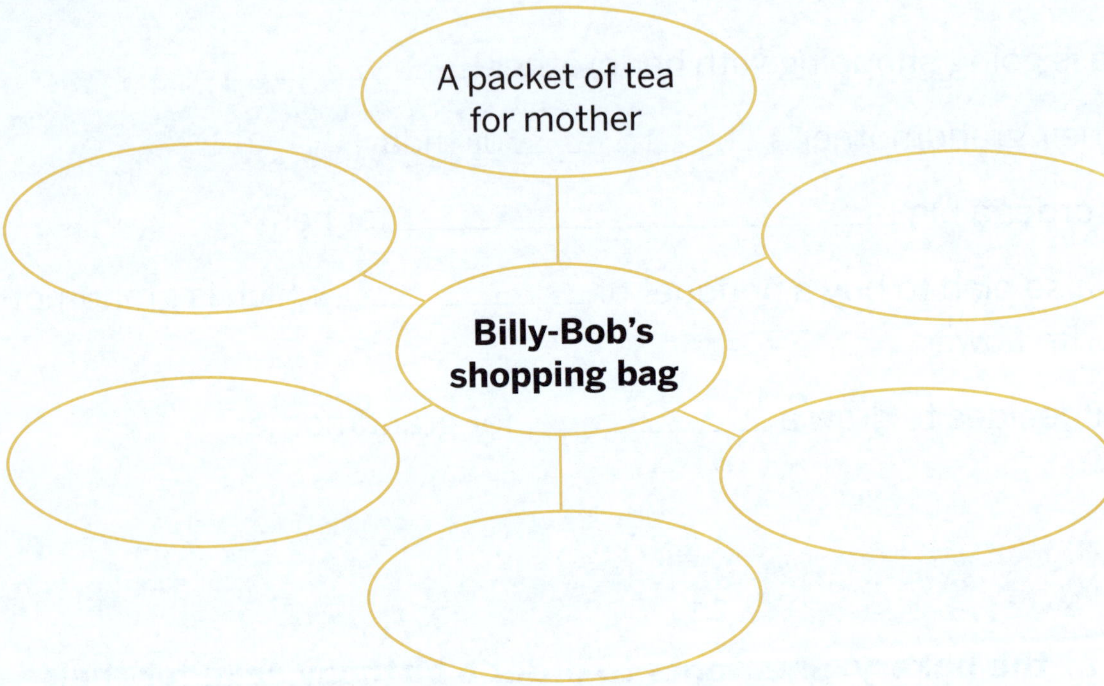

B Rewrite this paragraph using capital letters where needed.

my name is feroze. i am ten years old. i live in mumbai with my mother and father, my little sister and our pet cat, fluffy. my sister's name is mira. mira likes watching films. her favourite film is mr bean.

Unit 10

Here We Come

Vocabulary

A Fill in the blanks with the correct homophone.

1. They are waiting for ______________ (their/there) mother.
2. This toy is very ______________ (dear/deer) to her.
3. I will give you ______________ (too/two) candies if you answer correctly.
4. The ______________ (sun/son) is hidden behind the clouds.
5. We should take care of ______________ (hour/our) pets.
6. She bought ______________ (too/two) books from the bookshop.
7. I cannot ______________ (bear/bare) this cold anymore.
8. Let's ______________ (meat/meet) for dinner tonight.

B Match the beginning of each sentence with its ending.

1. I keep my clothes in	a. my desk.
2. The children were all asleep in	b. the table.
3. My father was sitting in	c. my wardrobe.
4. We always have dinner at	d. the cupboard, please?
5. Could you get the plates out of	e. their beds.
6. At school, I put my books on	f. his favourite armchair.

Grammar

Remember!

- Some words or sentences are used to give order or command.

  Please take your seat. *Close the windows.*

  Pour me a glass of milk. *Put that down now!*

A Look at the pictures and write the correct commands in the blanks.

Brush your teeth Please keep quiet Raise your hand

1. ____________

2. ____________

3. ____________

B Complete the sentences with the correct words or phrases.

Don't forget Don't listen Pass Pour Shut Take Turn Wash

1. ____________ me the salt, please.
2. ____________ right at the traffic light.
3. ____________ the juice into the glass.
4. ____________ to take your water bottle.
5. ____________ to that music. It is terrible.
6. ____________ the kettle before you use it.
7. ____________ the door, please. It's very cold.
8. ____________ an umbrella with you. It is raining.

Language skills

Read this to your partner. Pay special attention to the words with *sh* and *ch* sound and make sure that you pronounce them differently.

Writing

Put the words in the correct order to make sentences that contain suggestions. Remember to use capital letters and full stops or question marks.

1. come with/may we/you

____

2. a/let's have/picnic

____

3. join you in/may we/the park

____

4. bring my/I can/tennis rackets

____

5. invite Rakesh/let's/to the party

____

Activity 2

Listening

A **Listen to the words. Circle the word in each set that sounds different.**

	a.	b.	c.	d.
1.	a. can	b. fun	c. run	d. sun
2.	a. ball	b. call	c. full	d. wall
3.	a. carry	b. hurry	c. scurry	d. worry
4.	a. block	b. look	c. rock	d. sock
5.	a. blow	b. hoe	c. snow	d. too
6.	a. leave	b. like	c. light	d. smile

B **Listen and colour.**

Speaking

A **Look at the pictures and talk about them. Then read the dialogue and act it out.**

Gulab: Hi, Mum. I'm hungry.

Mum: OK, you can have two biscuits, but don't eat any more.

Gulab: Thanks, Mum.

Mum: I mean it. No more biscuits. We have guests coming for tea.

Gulab: I understand. Two biscuits are enough for me.

(Mum leaves the kitchen)

Gulab: Yummy! Those biscuits were good. I will have just one more. Mmmm, and another ... and another ... Oh no! There are no more biscuits!

(Mum enters the kitchen)

Mum: Oh, no! Gulab, there are no more biscuits! I told you ...

Gulab: Sorry, Mum!

Mum: Gulab! I am very angry with you.

B **Look at the pictures and say what is different.**

This snowman has got a scarf in Picture A. That snowman hasn't got a scarf in Picture B.

Picture A

Picture B

Test 2

Reading comprehension

A **Read this story about a beetle.**

The Singing Beetle

Poppy was a beetle who liked to sing. She sang if she was happy. She sang if she was sad.

The other beetles did not like Poppy singing. They said her singing was squeaky[1]. No one wanted to play with Poppy. Poppy was sad.

One day she went away into the forest. 'Now I can sing as loudly as I want. No one can hear me,' she said.

In the bush nearby was Harry, the mouse. Harry was hungry and he was looking for something to eat. In another bush was Jake, the snake. He was looking for something to eat, too.

Jake saw Harry and he was happy. 'Yummy, a mouse!' he said. Then Poppy saw Jake, the snake. She squeaked, 'Look out, Mouse! Snake wants to eat you!'

Harry saw the snake and ran to hide. He was quiet and did not move. Then Poppy began to sing in a very loud and squeaky voice. Jake, the snake, heard Poppy singing and he was afraid. He slid[2] away.

Harry came out and said to Poppy, 'You are a brave beetle. I like your singing. I like singing too. Let us sing together.'

So Poppy and Harry became friends and they sang together every day.

Linda Strachan

Wordfile

1. When someone speaks or sings making short, high sounds, it is known as **squeaky**.
2. When someone **slides**, he or she moves quickly and smoothly over a surface. Slid is the past tense of slide.

B **Put the words in the correct order to write the sentences from the story in your notebook. Remember to use capital letters and full stops.**

1. a beetle/Poppy/was

____

2. Poppy liked/the time/to sing all

____

3. did not like/her voice/Poppy's friends

____

4. and a snake/in the forest/there was a mouse

____

5. the mouse/the snake/wanted to eat

____

6. slid towards/the mouse/the snake

____

7. and warned/Poppy/saw/the mouse/the snake

____

8. from danger/Poppy/saved Harry

____

Coursebook Comprehension

Choose the best ending for each sentence.

1. In 'The Boy and the Drum', the boy wants to
   a. play with a guitar.
   b. play with a drum.
   c. play with a ball.
2. In 'Let's Build a Rocket', the girl wants to go on a trip with her friends
   a. in a boat.
   b. in a rocket.
   c. in a plane.
3. In part 1 of 'The Shepherd Boy', Nandu shouted 'WOLF!' because
   a. he saw a wolf.
   b. he was bored.
   c. he wanted to talk to people from the village.
4. In part 2 of 'The Shepherd Boy', Nandu really does see a wolf, and
   a. the villagers come to save him.
   b. he has to stay on the tree all night.
   c. his brother chases the wolf away.
5. In part 1 'Limerick', the ape is in
   a. the jungle.
   b. the park.
   c. the zoo.
6. In 'A Busy Morning', Billy-Bob was
   a. a helpful boy.
   b. a naughty boy.
   c. a wise boy.

7. In 'A Child's Song', the child is
   a. greedy and prays for more.
   b. ungrateful and always complains.
   c. grateful for the things she has in her life.
8. In 'Here We Come', every year Pitki and her parents
   a. went on vacations to different countries.
   b. went on mountain trekking.
   c. went to her grandparents' house in Assam.

Grammar

Answer the questions.

1. Complete the sentences with the correct form of the doing word in brackets.
   a. We can't go for a walk because it's __________ (rain).
   b. I talked to my friends and we __________ (decide) to go to the cinema.
   c. Amit __________ (want) to play cricket with us yesterday.
   d. Did you __________ (finish) your homework?
   e. We __________ (visit) our cousins in Australia last winter.
2. Underline the describing words in these sentences.
   a. Raj is very tall and strong.
   b. This suitcase is empty, so it isn't very heavy.
   c. The movie was very scary.
   d. Leena is a very friendly and helpful girl.
   e. The children were very calm and quiet when the teacher was in class.
   f. We camped under the large oak tree near the little stream.
3. Tick (✓) the correct sentence in each pair.
   a. I every day go to school. ☐ I go to school every day. ☐
   b. Neha often goes to Pooja's house. ☐
      Neha often to Pooja's house goes. ☐

Writing

A **Change the words in brackets to the past tense to complete the story.**

Yusuf and Kulbir went to visit their friend, Kaustav. They 1__________ (arrive) at 10:00 a.m., but Kaustav 2__________ (not be) there. They 3__________ (try) to call him on his mother's mobile phone. Kaustav was at the market, but he 4__________ (hurry) back at once.

First, the boys 5__________ (listen) to music, then they went to the park to play football. Kaustav's mother 6__________ (cook) a delicious lunch for them.

B **Look at the picture and write a few sentences describing the picture. You may use the hints given in the box.**

picnic with friends

tasty food

sunny weather

play with friends

yummy cake

____

____

____

____

____

____